by

Peter Webster

DICK WHITTINGTON
A pantomime in 2 acts

First Published in Great Britain in 2020 by Beercott Books.

Copyright: © Peter Webster 2020
ISBN: 978-1-9163953-0-5

Peter Webster has asserted his rights to be identified
as the author of this book.

Title is fully protected under copyright. All rights, including professional and amateur stage production, recitation, lecturing, public reading, motion picture, radio broadcasting, television and the rights of translation into foreign languages are strictly reserved.

A catalogue record of this book is available from the British Library.

No one shall make any changes to the play for the purpose of production. No part of this book may be reproduced, stored in a retrieval system, or transmitted in any form, by any means, now known or yet to be invented. This includes mechanical, electronic, photocopying, recording, videotaping, or otherwise, without the prior written permission of the publisher. No one shall upload this title, or part of this title, to social media websites.

Professional and amateur producers are hereby warned that title is subject to a licensing fee. Publication of this play does not imply availability for performance. Both amateurs and professionals considering a production are strongly advised to apply to the agent before starting rehearsals, advertising, or booking a theatre. A licence fee must be paid whether the title is presented for charity or gain and whether or not admission is charged.

Worldwide licence enquiries for this title should be directed to:
licensing@beercottbooks.co.uk.
Title subject to availability.

---

www.beercottbooks.co.uk

Beercott

CHARATERS

DICK WHITTINGTON – our hero
CALICO – Dick's cat
ALDERMAN FITZWARREN – Dick's employer
ALICE FITZWARREN – his adopted daughter
PHOBIA FITZWARREN – his wife
TAPIOCA DRIPPING – Fitzwarren's cook
CAPTAIN COCKLESHELL – the ship's captain
SALTY SWAB – the ship's first mate
SNITCH – the Chief Rat
BOHO – the King of Barbary
BLACK BERRY – the pirate captain
Chorus of: townspeople, courtiers, rats, cats and pirates

A note: A 'calico cat' is another name for a tortoiseshell, and is seen as lucky in some societies. Some stage directions have been provided for Calico, but whoever plays him will have to react to everything said and done on stage, in as catlike way as possible.

SCENES

ACT ONE

SCENE ONE: The town square (*Main stage*)
SCENE TWO: A road leading to the harbour (*Lower stage/half tabs*)
SCENE THREE: The town square (*Main stage*)
SCENE FOUR: A quiet place (*Lower stage/half tabs*)
SCENE FIVE: The galley of the Unicorn (*Main stage*)
SCENE SIX: Another quiet place (*Lower stage/half tabs*)
SCENE SEVEN: The town square (*Main stage*)

ACT TWO

SCENE ONE: The town square (*Main stage*)
SCENE TWO: On Highgate hill (*Lower stage/half tabs*)
SCENE THREE: Aboard the Unicorn (*Main stage*)
SCENE FOUR: Below decks (*Lower stage/half tabs*)
SCENE FIVE: The King's palace (*Main stage*)

ACT ONE
Scene One

Overture of songs used during the show; directors are free to make their own choice of songs and to decide their place in the action. As the overture ends the curtains open to the town square and the chorus go straight into their opening song. At this point everyone is on stage except FITZWARREN, ALICE, TAPIOCA, PHOBIA, CAPTAIN COCKLESHELL and SALTY SWAB; DICK and CALICO are on stage but unseen, as they are both sitting slumped at the back of the stage, hidden by the crowd. As the song ends the crowd parts, so that DICK and CALICO are now in view.

1ST CITIZEN: Here! Who are you? And what are you doing cluttering up our nice tidy part of London Town?

2ND CITIZEN: And does that cat belong to you? Great hairy thing! Bet it's got fleas.

DICK: Well, that's a fine welcome for two tired strangers, I must say. *(CALICO nods in agreement.)* Anyway, what's your problem? We're not doing any harm.

1ST CITIZEN: I told you; you're making the place look untidy....

2ND CITIZEN: And you're up to no good, I'll be bound.

DICK: Look, just leave us alone; we'll have our rest and then we'll be on our way.

3RD CITIZEN: Well I say, lock 'em up! They can have a nice long rest in gaol. *(General assent from the crowd; CALICO shakes his head in disbelief.)*

4TH CITIZEN: We won't be able to sleep securely in our beds with all these strangers about.

DICK: All these strangers? One boy and a cat?

1ST CITIZEN: And I need my beauty sleep.

2ND CITIZEN: *(To 1ST CITIZEN.)* Too right you do! With your looks you need all the sleep you can get! *(General laughter.)*

1ST CITIZEN: Just say that again!

2ND CITIZEN: *(Squaring up to 1ST CITIZEN.)* You could sleep for a week, but it wouldn't improve your looks!

1ST CITIZEN: Why you.....

DICK: *(Butting in.)* Alright! Alright! We're going before anyone gets hurt! *(DICK and CALICO get up and start gathering their few possessions; then sarcastically.)* Thank you all so much for your hospitality. And, don't worry – we won't be back! *(DICK turns to go while CALICO, in his turn, performs the most sarcastic bow he can think of.)*

ALL: Good riddance! *(Alice enters.)*

ALICE: What on earth is going on? What's all this noise?

3RD CITIZEN: *(Pointing to DICK and CALICO.)* It's these two, miss. Strangers, up to no good. We've told them to move on.

ALICE: Why, what have they done?

1ST CITIZEN: Well nothing – yet.

ALICE: Then that's hardly fair! Has everyone forgotten their manners? *(Looking DICK and CALICO up and down.)* They don't seem to be much of a threat to me. Just two tired and hungry fellow beings.

DICK: That's exactly what we are; no more and no less.

ALICE: *(Turning to the crowd.)* You should be ashamed of yourselves! How would you like to be a stranger in a strange town? *(The crowd look sheepish. Then to DICK.)* Now, let me fetch my father, he'll know what to do with you. *(ALICE shouts into the wings.)* Father! Please come here a moment, we need your advice! *(After a short pause, FITZWARREN, PHOBIA and TAPIOCA enter.)*

FITZWARREN: What is it my dear? We were in the middle of planning next week's menus.

PHOBIA: Yes; mince, mince and more mince! *(To TAPIOCA.)* Call yourself a cook?

TAPIOCA: It's not my fault; I've only got to page one in my recipe book.

ALICE: *(Indicating DICK and CALICO.)* This boy and his cat are strangers here; they're tired and hungry and no one knows what to do with them.

1ST CITIZEN: I know what I'd do with them, if I had my way!

FITZWARREN: *(To all in general.)* Please be quiet while I sort this out. *(Turning to DICK.)* What's your name boy?

DICK: Dick. Dick Whittington.

FITZWARREN: And where have you come from?

DICK: We've run away from the poorhouse; we've been walking for days.

PHOBIA: Run away from the poorhouse, eh? Why, I wonder? Best place for your type.

DICK: It's simple – there was no food. And no future either. I decided I'd rather take my chances in the wide world, than stay there and rot.

TAPIOCA: But where are your parents, dear?

DICK: I'm an orphan; that's why I was in the poorhouse. This cat *(Indicating CALICO.)* is my only friend.

TAPIOCA: And why did you come here, to London?

DICK: Everyone told me that London was the place to make your fortune – that the streets were paved with gold. *(Everyone falls about laughing.)* I haven't seen much gold so far. I feel such a fool. *(CALICO tugs DICK'S hand for attention and whispers in his ear.)*

ALICE: Just a minute! Did your cat talk to you? What did he say?

DICK: He said 'I told you so'.

TAPIOCA: That cat's got more sense than you have.

ALICE: Father, can't we help him? Can't you find a job for him?

PHOBIA: What? And take in every waif and stray who turns up on our doorstep?

FITZWARREN: Hush dear. Now Dick, tell me what you can do that might help you earn a living?

DICK: I can read and write, and I can keep books; I can cook and sew a bit. At least they taught us useful stuff in the poorhouse. And I'm good with my hands.

PHOBIA: Yes, helping yourself to other people's goods I suppose.

ALICE: Mother! That's very unfair! Just because he's poor doesn't mean he steals.

DICK: No, no, the lady is right to be suspicious – but I've never taken anything that wasn't mine.

TAPIOCA: If there's anyone around here with sticky fingers it's me; it's all that treacle!

FITZWARREN: I'd like to believe you lad, and it just so happens that I need someone I can trust to help me plan my voyages and to keep track of everything in the cargos. In fact, you can start today!

DICK: Thank you sir, you're very kind; but do you have a place for my cat? I couldn't bear to part with him. *(CALICO falls at FITZWARREN'S feet and clasps his paws in pleading.)*

PHOBIA: Can a cat read? Can it write? It's no use to us. Get rid of it – nasty, hairy beast! One stray is enough to take in.

ALICE: Surely he can be useful somehow? *(CALICO again tugs DICK'S hand and meows in his ear.)* Now what's he saying?

DICK: He says that if you've a problem with rats or mice, he can solve it.

TAPIOCA: I've got an idea! He's a cat – just what I need to solve the problem of all the rats and mice that keep getting into my pantry and making off with the cheese! *(CALICO gets up and performs a pounce.)*

FITZWARREN: But what about all the traps you set for them?

TAPIOCA: Oh these rats are too clever for traps. They steal the cheese out of them and then hide the traps in my bed. And when I climb in, all ready for my beddy byes, off go the traps. Snap! Snap! Snap! My poor toes are black and blue.

DICK: Don't worry, he'll get rid of your rats, I promise you. There wasn't a single mouse or rat left in the poorhouse by the time he'd finished. *(CALICO gestures like a prize fighter.)*

ALICE: And he can be useful on your ships Father; he can chase the rats overboard.

PHOBIA: More likely, they'll make him walk the plank! Have you seen the size of them?

FITZWARREN: *(To DICK, ignoring her.)* How are his sea legs?

DICK: Fine, absolutely fine! He's an old sea dog – I mean cat! *(Unseen by FITZWARREN, CALICO mimes throwing up.)*

ALICE: *(Taking CALICO'S paws.)* Does this cat of yours have a name? What do we call him?

DICK: Yes, he has a name. It's Calico.

TAPIOCA: That's funny name. Is that fur really cotton? Can I make a dress out of him?

DICK: No! No! It's very simple; a cat with the name of Calico is supposed to bring good luck.

PHOBIA: I hope for your sake that that's true.

FITZWARREN: Now, now, dear – we can't judge a book by its cover – or in this case, a cat by its fur. But now we must get on with our preparations for the next voyage. The first job is to lay in some provisions. Now, where's my captain and first mate? They should be here by now. *(He goes to the wings and shouts.)* Cockleshell! Swab! Where are you? Come here at once!

COCKLESHELL: *(Offstage.)* Coming Sir, coming!

SWAB: *(Offstage.)* On our way Sir! On our way! *(There is a short pause before they appear, slightly the worse for wear.)*

FITZWARREN: Where have you been? You're late!

COCKLESHELL: Sorry Sir; we had go by the brewery to supervise the filling of the beer barrels.

SWAB: And of course, it was our duty to check the quality of the beer.

FITWARREN: *(Sarcastically.)* I trust it was up to scratch. What a dedicated pair you are. What would I do without you?

COCKLESHELL: *(Oblivious to all this.)* All in a day's work. Now Sir, what are your orders?

SWAB: Don't forget we haven't checked the hammocks for comfort. You don't want any lumps in your hammock!

TAPIOCA: The only lumps in a hammock are you two! All that gets you out of bed is the sun going over the yardarm; and then it's straight into the Sailors Rest!

FITWARREN: That's enough! There's work to be done. *(To COCKLESHELL and SWAB.)* Your first job is to pick up some sacks of flour from the miller and put them in the ships' galley. Be quick about it!

COCKLESHELL: Aye, aye, Sir! And where do we get the horse and cart?

PHOBIA: You don't! They're too expensive. You'll have to carry them.

COCKLESHELL: Carry them? But, but, but – I've got a bad back.

SWAB: And I've got a bad leg.

FITZWARREN: You'll both have a bad date if you're not careful – down at the job centre!

ALICE: You'll be all washed up!

TAPIOCA: All at sea!

PHOBIA: Up the creek without a paddle!

DICK: I could help. I don't mind fetching and carrying. Nor does Calico. *(CALICO indicates that this is not the case at all.)*

FITZWARREN: No Dick, thank you. I've got more important work for you. These two lazybones will just have to weigh their anchors and get on with it. Now, come on everyone! The work won't wait!

FITZWARREN leads everyone offstage, but ALICE quickly turns to DICK, puts a finger to her lips for silence and holds him back. CALICO turns to go with the others, but noticing this, stops to listen. When all have gone.

ALICE: There's something I want to tell you....

DICK: *(Interrupting her.)* I can't thank you enough for helping me. I was at my wits end. No money, nowhere to live and no prospects. *(CALICO watches and listens to all that follows.)*

Act 1 DICK WHITTINGTON 11

ALICE: Listen to me! You and Calico turning up has brightened my day no end. I like you and I think you and I can be friends – and I really need a friend.

DICK: I don't understand! You're an alderman's daughter – surely you must have everything you want.

ALICE: But I'm not his daughter – I'm an orphan like you. I'm adopted and my so-called mother never lets me forget it. To her I'm just an expensive nuisance – she treats me like a servant. Do this, do that! Never time for myself.

DICK: But doesn't your father stop her?

ALICE: He doesn't see what's going on – he's too busy with his ships and cargos. I don't want to tell him how she treats me, he's got enough to worry about. But now you're here, I've got someone to talk to – someone who understands how I feel. That's a comfort to me.

DICK: I just hope that I can live up to that. I'll do what I can – trust me.

ALICE: *(Realising time is passing.)* Enough talk – I've already said too much. We must go before we're missed!

As they exit, CALICO rubs his paws in a knowing way, then follows them offstage.

Curtain.

Scene Two

On the 'road to the harbour', in front of half tabs or on a lower stage. COCKLESHELL and SALTY enter down the centre aisle, each staggering under the weight of sacks of flour; they complain bitterly as they approach the stage.

COCKLESHELL: This stuff weighs a ton, I'm nearly on my knees and we've only been going five minutes. It's no wonder Tapioca's cakes never rise – the flour's just too heavy!

SALTY: It's a pity it's not self-raising – then we wouldn't have to struggle so much to lift it.

COCKLESHELL: True – that really would be flour power. *(By now they have reached the stage.)* Anyway, I need a rest! *(He drops his sack to the floor and sits on it.)* That's much better! *(SALTY does the same.)*

SALTY: I think it's very cruel of the boss not to let us have a horse and cart.

COCKLESHELL: That decision's just not horse sense.

SALTY: And I didn't sign up for this voyage to be a beast of burden. You told me the fresh sea air would do me good. Well that's just a load of hot air.

COCKLESHELL: Well, you should have read the terms and conditions, especially that bit about air conditioning.

SALTY: Any more of this and I shall lose my cool!

COCKLESHELL: Do I sense a chill in our relationship? *(While they have been talking, the rats have been creeping up on them, closing in from all sides. Sensing that something is wrong, COCKLESHELL moves closer to SALTY.)* Here, Salty! Don't look now, but I think there's someone else here – we've been caught cold. *(The rats suddenly move in, surrounding COCKLESHELL and SALTY.)*

SNITCH: You certainly have! Good day to you Captain. *(COCKLESHELL and SALTY jump up and cling onto each other for support, knees knocking. Then, peering at the sacks.)* And it looks like you've brought us a present. How very generous! Now I wonder what it could be?

1ST RAT: Maybe it's some coal – just what we want to keep us nice and warm in the winter.

2ND RAT: Maybe it's some smart new clothes, so that we can go out on the town.

SNITCH: *(Sniffing the sacks.)* No boys, it's better than that, it's flour! Pancakes for tea tonight! Thank you so much; very thoughtful of you both.

COCKLESHELL: But, but, it's not for you! It's supplies for our next voyage; we've got to get it on board the good ship The Unicorn.

SALTY: We'll be keel hauled if we don't.

SNITCH: It'll be the rat o' nine tails if you do! Listen, we'll do you a favour – weren't you complaining just now about how heavy those sacks are?

COCKLESHELL: Yes, but....

1ST RAT: We'll do the carrying from now on.

2ND RAT: Save you the trouble.

SNITCH: Exactly! So be good boys and make yourselves scarce. *(Waving them away.)*

1ST RAT: Or do we have to be a bit more persuasive>

2ND RAT: We're very good at persuading!

COCKLESHELL: No, no, you've convinced us!

SALTY: We couldn't be more convinced!

SNITCH: At the risk of repeating myself – make yourselves scarce*!* *(The rats start to close in still further on COCKLESHELL and SALTY, who beat a hasty and undignified retreat. The triumphal rats watch them go and then settle themselves on the sacks.)* Good going boys. Nicely done as usual; we'll eat well tonight.

1ST RAT: Maybe have a few drinks as well.

2ND RAT: Yeah, we'll get ratted!

SNITCH: Ain't we just the smartest, shiftiest, most devious set of rats in town?

1ST RAT: Nothing and no one's safe from us.

2ND RAT: Never seen and never heard.

SNITCH: True boys – no one can put a finger on us! *(Meanwhile DICK and CALICO enter unnoticed by the rats; DICK bends and whispers in CALICO'S ear, who nods in agreement.)*

DICK: Maybe not a finger – but how about a claw? Get 'em Calico!

SNITCH: Help! A cat! Run for it boys! Every rat for himself!

CALICO rushes in amongst the rats who scatter, to shouts of "help", "keep him away from me", "watch out for those paws", "it's a catastrophe", "don't get in a catflap" etc. When all the rats have disappeared, there are a few moments of quiet, then DICK goes to CALICO and puts an arm around his shoulder.

DICK: Well done my friend! You really gave them what for. Now, we've got to get this flour to The Unicorn and then report back to base. *(DICK picks up the sacks, seemingly with ease, and he and CALICO exit.)*

Scene Three

The curtains open to the town square; ALICE follows PHOBIA onto the stage.

PHOBIA: Haven't you finished your work yet? What have you been doing all this time?

ALICE: I've been washing the floors and laying the fires, just as you told me. And yes, I've just finished.

PHOBIA: Good; then there's a few more little jobs you can be getting on with. There's a week's washing and ironing to be done – and someone's got to go with Tapioca to carry the shopping.

ALICE: Oh, please! No more jobs. I haven't had a moment to myself since I got up.

PHOBIA: So? What else should you be doing? You've got to earn your keep, and a little hard work won't harm you.

FITZWARREN and TAPIOCA enter.

FITZWARREN: Hello my dears; having a nice chat?

ALICE: Yes Father, we were just…..

PHOBIA: *(Cutting in.)* ….planning our next little trip to the shops and discussing how we can keep up with all the latest fashions.

TAPIOCA: The latest fashions? Easy – you just have to take your cue from me. Style icon and trendsetter, that's me! *(She is, of course, the antithesis of a style icon.)*

PHOBIA: Oh I see; we should all resemble an explosion in a paint factory? Well then, I've certainly got some catching up to do.

FITZWARREN: Good, good! I'm glad you're enjoying yourselves, but we have to get on; time and tide wait for no man. Which reminds me, Captain Cockleshell and Salty should be back by now.

PHOBIA: I wouldn't hold your breath; knowing them, they've gone off chasing mermaids again. They believe anything you tell them.

ALICE: *(Looking offstage.)* No, it's alright; here they come now.

COCKLESHELL and SALTY enter, looking very sheepish; they are followed by the citizens who react to the following dialogue.

FITZWARREN: *(To COCKLESHELL and SALTY.)* At last! Where have you been? You should have been here hours ago!

COCKLESHELL: We would have been here sooner, but we got held up.

TAPIOCA: Oh, yes? Did you have to wait while they brought up another barrel from the cellar at the Sailor's Rest?

SALTY: No, no, no! We were really held up, waylaid, robbed!

FITZWARREN: Robbed? Who by? There are no highwaymen round here!

PHOBIA: What did I tell you? These two are as much use as the proverbial chocolate tea pot.

COCKLESHELL: They were highway rats not highwaymen.

FITZWARREN: What? Explain yourselves! Now!

COCKLESHELL: We'd stopped for a little rest....

SALTY: And then we were ambushed....

COCKLESHELL: By a swarm of rats....

SALTY: Hundreds of rats!

TAPIOCA: Hundreds of rats? Nonsense! You pair of moaning mariners!

ALICE: Be honest – how many were there really?

COCKLESHELL: Er – thirty.

SALTY: Twenty.

COCKLESHELL: Well, several anyway.

PHOBIA: I see no bruises, no broken bones. You obviously put up quite a fight.

SALTY: Oh, we did, we did!

COCKLESHELL: And now we're at the end of our tether. We're quite worn out.

Act 1   DICK WHITTINGTON   17

FITZWARREN: I'm not worried about you two! What's happened to my flour?

COCKLESHELL: Last seen, it was under a heap of rats.

ALICE: So, that's the last we'll see of it.

TAPIOCA: But that's a disaster! That means a long sea voyage with no bread; and worse still, no cakes to help keep up my morale. And my morale needs a lot of keeping up! *(DICK and CALICO enter.)*

DICK: Don't worry Mrs Dripping – you'll get your bread and cakes!

ALICE: What do you mean Dick? Have you bought some more flour?

PHOBIA: Oh, yes? And where did you get the money for that?

DICK: No, no, we didn't buy it – we rescued it from those pesky rats. Calico and I followed these two. *(Pointing to COCKLESHELL and SALTY.)* We thought they might get into trouble of some sort – and sure enough, they did. We came across the rats, sitting on their spoils. Calico employed a little gentle persuasion to scare them and make them give the flour back. So we picked up the sacks, took them to the harbour and put them safely aboard the good ship The Unicorn.

FITZWARREN: Well, thank you Dick. It seems we may have underestimated you and Calico – well done, both of you! You've certainly repaid my confidence. *(CALICO preens at this.)*

ALICE: Yes, you certainly have. There's more to you two than meets the eye.

PHOBIA: *(Aside.)* Yes indeed, very impressive. I wonder....

FITZWARREN: Now that problem has been overcome, we can get ready to set off on our voyage to the kingdom of Barbary. Now, where did I put that list of possible cargo? *(He pulls a parchment from his pocket.)* Now let's think; what do people need when they live in a very hot country? What should we put on board? *(He scrutinises his list.)* Fur coats – tick;

umbrellas – tick; chilli peppers – tick; nutty slack – tick; ice skates – tick. And I suppose we could include some nice woolly blankets. That should do the trick – this trip should make us rich! Now, everybody go and pack what you need; *(As he goes.)* Oh, and Tapioca, you'd better get cooking and lay in some supplies. We'll need plenty of sustaining food!
(Curtain, as everyone follows FITZWARREN off stage.)

Act 1   DICK WHITTINGTON   19

Scene Four

A quiet place; in front of half tabs or on a lower stage. PHOBIA enters.

PHOBIA: Oh yes, that was certainly impressive; that cat could be worth a fortune in the right hands. And that means my hands, of course. (*She ponders the problem, pacing the stage.*) Now, let me think; that cat obviously has a talent for dealing with rats, so I need to find somewhere overrun with rats or...... better still, recruit my own rats to do the overrunning! Yes, that's it! And then when I get to this place, wherever it is, I offer to rid it of the rats in exchange for a nice fat fee; all I've got to do is find a way of kidnapping that cat, and then force it to do the necessary. And that'll be easy peasy, 'cos I'll pay the rats to be got rid of. Genius! And when the job is done, I collect my money and walk away. And I can repeat my little scam in loads of places and no one will be any the wiser. Now, where would I go to find someone who would be willing to pay a fortune to get rid of a few pesky rats? It has to be far away from here, and somewhere where the emperor or king, or whatever, is very, very rich. I know! The land of Barbary! That's why Fitzwarren wants to trade there. If I can get there first, I'll be the one to do the trading – and I'll definitely be trading up! (*She pauses to reflect.*) But it gets better, oh yes, so much better. Fitzwarren is much too honest for his own good, he'll never make a fortune. The fortune I so richly deserve! So when he gets to Barbary, he'll find I've cornered the market. I'll make my fortune, but he'll be ruined and better still so will his precious Alice. Just think of it – both of them homeless while I build myself a mansion, load myself with jewels and leave Fitzwarren and all this grubby commerce behind. Delicious! But first I need to find some rats willing to join me in this nice little scam. (*She thinks.*) That Snitch and his boys should fit the bill – when it comes to dirty tricks, they're the tops; they've certainly had their uses in the past. And they owe me a big favour after I tipped them off about the flour delivery. (*She searches in her pocket for a small set of pipes and plays a short, haunting, tune. There is the sound of scuffling as once again the rats appear from various parts of the theatre and gather round her.*)

SNITCH: What do you want this time? Nothing good, I'll be bound. Oh, and by the way, thanks so much for the tip off – shame you didn't warn us about that cat!

1ST RAT: He was a nasty surprise and no mistake; when it came to handing out punishment he was the cat's whiskers!

2ND RAT: Ruined our nice little plan – he really put the cat among the pigeons! I've still got the bruises.

1ST RAT: And we lost our supper.

2ND RAT: So we're still hungry!

SNITCH: Are you going to compensate us or do we let the cat out of the bag about what you've been up to?

PHOBIA: Boys! Boys! You can't blame me – I knew nothing about that cat; he just turned up out of the blue. But – there's a way you can get your revenge.

SNITCH: Oh yeah? How?

1ST RAT: And does it involve getting scared to death?

2ND RAT: And what's in it for us?

PHOBIA: Come here and I'll tell you. How do you feel about a nice sea cruise, with no risk of having to desert a sinking ship? *(PHOBIA and the rats go into a huddle and as she whispers to them we hear the occasional word of explanation such as: 'scam', 'overrun', 'Barbary', 'deal', 'kidnap', 'pretend', 'fortune'. As they move apart.)*

SNITCH: I like it! Count us in!

1ST RAT: When do we start?

PHOBIA: As soon as possible; we've got to get to sea before Fitzwarren, so we get to Barbary first.

2ND RAT: And what's our share going to be?

SNITCH: Yeah, we want the biggest cut as we're the ones risking our necks!

PHOBIA: Fair enough; how about sixty percent?

SNITCH: That's not enough!

PHOBIA: Alright – fifty percent.

1ST RAT: No, forty percent!

2ND RAT: Higher! Thirty percent!

PHOBIA: Done!

SNITCH: *(Thoroughly confused.)* I'm not sure, but I think we have been.

PHOBIA: Enough talk; we've plans to make and a kid to catnap. No, I mean a cat to kidnap.

All exit.

Scene Five

> *The galley of the Unicorn; on stage are TAPIOCA, DICK and CALICO. There is a table on which is set a very large cookery book, tins and jars of 'ingredients' and also a large bowl. There is a second bowl hidden inside the large bowl; this contains 'custard pie' foam. This arrangement leaves space for the ingredients to be placed between the edges of the two bowls. There is also a large, old fashioned, oven with an opening door. ALICE enters carrying a pile of assorted parcels which she can hardly see over; she barges into the table, dropping the parcels. She stoops to pick them up.*

ALICE: Sorry, sorry! My fault, sorry!

TAPIOCA: I don't know what it is about you my girl, but sometimes you don't half remind me of my little one. She was forever falling over and dropping things; if there was a glass of water anywhere in range she'd find a way of knocking it over. I spent half my life mopping up after her.

DICK: I don't want to pry, but what happened to her?

TAPIOCA: I hadn't a penny to my name so they split us up – me to the poorhouse and her to an orphanage!

DICK: I'm sorry, I didn't mean to....

TAPIOCA: So am I, but enough talk, we've got work to do. *(Turning over the pages of the book. Her tone changes.)* I've just acquired this at great expense; it's Mary Currant's latest cook book.

ALICE: What's it called? And is there any chance it'll improve your cooking?

TAPIOCA: Cheek! It's called 'Quick recipes for starving sailors'.

DICK: Crew cuts in other words – very useful.

TAPIOCA: We need to get on, lots to do; we can start by making some cakes and you can all help. Let's see. *(Turning the pages.)* Ah, here we are! How to make a sponge cake. *(She reads.)* First take forty zeds of butter.

ALICE: Forty zeds? Are you sure? I don't understand.

Act 1   DICK WHITTINGTON   23

DICK: Let me look. No, silly, it says four ozes! *(He pronounces it as 'aussies'.)*

ALICE: What have Australians got to do with it? *(CALICO makes a gesture of frustration, tugs DICK'S hand for attention and whispers in his ear.)*

DICK: Calico says we're all being very silly; it's not zeds or ozes – it's ounces. It's a measure of weight, so we'll need some scales. And anyway he says we can leave all this to him – it's under control.

TAPIOCA: Nonsense! What does a cat know about cooking? And what does he mean scales? We're not a choir.

ALICE: No, not notes! Scales! Those balance things you use to weigh stuff.

TAPIOCA: Oh, I see. Well we haven't got any, so I'll just have to guess. Now, where's that butter? *(She searches for butter without success.)* Bother, no butter!

DICK: *(Finding a jar.)* I've found some peanut butter.

TAPIOCA: That'll do; sounds like the same sort of stuff. It's butter isn't it? *(She spoons this into the bowl.)* What's next? *(Consulting the book.)* Four ounces of sugar. *(Finding a bag of sugar and tipping some into the bowl.)* In you go. Next! Four ounces of self-raising flour. *(Once again she searches without success.)* No self-raising! *(To DICK.)* Here, what's happened to all that flour you put in here?

DICK: I've no idea, someone must have used it already. *(CALICO points to himself, but all ignore him.)*

TAPIOCA: Nonsense, no one's done any cooking. It's a mystery. *(Spotting another bag.)* But what's this? Cornflour – that'll do! *(She tips this into the bowl.)*

ALICE: Are you sure? That doesn't sound right.

TAPIOCA: It's flour isn't it? Must do the same thing. *(All this time CALICO has been looking on, getting more and more exasperated. Once again he tugs at DICK'S hand and meows in his ear.)*

DICK: Calico says you're doing it all wrong and it'll be a disaster.

TAPIOCA: Rubbish! As I said, what does a cat know about cooking? Nothing! Where was I? *(Consulting the book; CALICO turns away in disgust.)* Two large eggs. *(Again she searches.)* No eggs! *(Coming across a packet and reading the label.)* Scotch eggs! They'll do – in they go.

ALICE: Is that everything? *(She looks at the book.)* No, one more thing – vanilla essence. What's that?

DICK: No idea – probably just to give it some flavour.

TAPIOCA: It's flavour that we want is it? This'll do the job; brown sauce – ideal. *(She picks up a large bottle of brown sauce and appears to tip this into the bowl. Then, looking at the book.)* 'Mix well and taste before cooking'. *(She takes a wooden spoon and appears to stir vigorously the contents of the bowl. After a few moments.)* That should do it! So, who wants a taste?

DICK/ALICE: I do! *(They dip wooden spoons into the mixture in the small bowl and appear to take a taste. Both choke and pull faces; CALICO makes a 'told you so' gesture.)* It's horrible! Are you trying to poison us?

TAPIOCA: Me? I was just following the recipe – I knew that Mary Currant was rubbish! Why don't you two do it, if you think you can do better?

DICK/ALICE: But you're supposed to be the cook!

TAPIOCA: Any more from you two and I shall go on strike!

ALICE: Good! Then we shan't have to eat any of your food.

Dick Or follow any of your so-called recipes!

TAPIOCA: Why, you cheeky little…… *(She takes some of the contents of the small bowl and flicks it at DICK and ALICE, who retaliate as soon as they can get their spoons into the small bowl. A full blown food fight develops. CALICO watches on in despair, but after a few seconds of mayhem he steps forward to separate the warring parties. Once again he tugs DICK'S hand and meows in his ear. A short pause.)*

DICK: Calico says we're all hopeless and if the crew have to rely on us during the voyage there'd be a mutiny and we'd be feeding the sharks not the crew. He also says that he thought he'd try his paw at cooking, so he did some earlier this morning and it should be ready now and would we like to see the result?

Tapioca, Alice and lastly, DICK, all stare at each other in disbelief and then nod and stand aside as CALICO goes to the oven, opens the door and removes a large and beautifully decorated cake. He places this on the table as the curtains slowly close, while TAPIOCA, ALICE and DICK stand by dumfounded.

Scene Six

A quiet place; in front of half tabs or on a lower stage. CAPTAIN COCKLESHELL and SALTY enter, pulling CALICO by his paws, closely followed by DICK.

DICK: *(As he enters.)* Hoi! Where are you taking Calico?

COCKLESHELL: To the ship of course; we've just press-ganged him so now he's part of the crew.

DICK: You can't do that! He can't go to sea!

COCKLESHELL: Oh yes, he can!

DICK: Oh no, he can't!

COCKLESHELL: Oh yes, he can! I bet he can get up the rigging a lot faster than you.

DICK: Maybe, but he's got no head for heights. *(CALICO staggers about as if dizzy.)* He'll fall overboard.

COCKLESHELL: Tough!

DICK: And he'll be sick all the time; he's never, ever, been to sea – he's got no sea paws. *(Once again, CALICO mimes spectacularly throwing up.)*

SALTY: No problem – I've got a bucket with his name on it. Or I would have if I could spell it! *(In the meantime, CALICO has tried to sneak away, only to be collared by the CAPTAIN.)*

COCKLESHELL: *(Talking directly to CALICO.)* No more excuses, you're coming with us. We'll soon knock you into shape.

SALTY: Yeah, shipshape! By the time we've finished with you you'll take the ship's biscuit.

DICK: But why has he got to come with us? What's so important?

COCKLESHELL: *(Still holding onto CALICO.)* Because he's your contribution to the success of this voyage. If you two want a share of the profits, he's going to help you earn it. *(He releases CALICO.)*

SALTY: And that's when your ship will come in!

COCKLESHELL: *(To DICK.)* So if <u>you</u> want to be rich, <u>he's</u> coming with <u>us.</u> *(FITZWARREN enters.)*

Act 1   DICK WHITTINGTON   27

FITZWARREN: Well Captain, is everything ready? Cargo loaded?

SALTY: Aye, aye, sir; all safely stowed.

FITZWARREN: All the necessary provisions on board?

COCKLESHELL: Everything we'll need.

FITZWARREN: And is your new crew all ready and eager to sail the bounding main?

COCKLESHELL: Ah, yes…..well……

SALTY: Just one teeny problem…..

FITZWARREN: What sort of problem? What about the crew?

COCKLESHELL: Ah, yes; the crew….

SALTY: Well you see it's like this….

FITZWARREN: Come on, out with it! Where's the crew?

COCKLESHELL: There isn't one.

SALTY: We're all out of jolly jack tars.

COCKLESHELL: We've scoured everywhere we could think of where we might find a crew.

DICK: Everywhere you could think of? That didn't take you two long then.

SALTY: No one was willing to sign on.

COCKLESHELL: It's all a bit of a shipwreck really.

DICK: Why would no one sign on? What's the problem?

FITZWARREN: *(Sarcastically.)* Yes do tell; I'd love to hear your excuses.

SALTY: They're afraid of pirates.

COCKLESHELL: They're afraid of sea monsters.

SALTY: Yes, ever since they watched Pirates Of The Caribbean.

COCKLESHELL: And they're really afraid of the Bermuda Triangle.

SALTY: Even though we told them Barry Manilow isn't on this cruise. *(Aside to the audience.)* You're all too young for that one.

COCKLESHELL: But the main reason is that you won't be paying them 'till the end of the voyage.

SALTY: And they've all been caught by that one before.

FITZWARREN: I can't help that; I can't pay them 'till I've been paid. Bit of a cash flow crisis.

DICK: Well what can we do now? No crew, no voyage.

FITZWARREN: There's only one thing for it; I'll have to recruit you, Alice, Tapioca and some of the townspeople as crew.

DICK: But none of us, apart from these two, *(Indicating COCKLESHELL and SALTY.)* knows how to sail a ship; and I'm not at all sure about them. We're all at sea when it comes to boats. *(CALICO once again tries to sneak away, but DICK grabs him.)*

FITZWARREN: We'll just have to learn fast! Come on all of you, we've got a crew to find! *(FITZWARREN leads them off, as the curtains open.)*

Act 1 DICK WHITTINGTON 29

Scene Seven

The town square. The stage is in darkness; the lights slowly come up to give a moonlight effect, gradually revealing a number of indistinct figures scattered about the stage (and possibly the lower stage, if there is one) – these turn out to be cats. CALICO is among them.

1ST CAT: Hoi, Calico! What's all this we hear about you going to sea? *(In the following dialogue the 'cat' is emphasised.)*

CALICO: Not my idea, didn't have any choice – it's just been a catalogue of disasters.

2ND CAT: Let's hope you don't fall overboard; we don't want you turning into a catfish do we?

CALICO: Oh, very funny! Don't make me any more nervous; I'm like a cat on hot bricks already.

3RD CAT: You know, once you've been at sea for a while, you won't be able to stand straight. You'll have a catalyst!

1ST CAT: Let's hope you don't meet any pirates; you could have a nasty attack of catarrh! *(The 'arrh' is emphasised of course.)*

2ND CAT: Could be catching! And if any blood is spilt, you'll be in a category all of your own. *(The 'gory' is emphasised as well.)*

CALICO: You know, you're not making me feel any better.

3RD CAT: And you're sure to get really seasick – a nasty case of catgut. That'll make you caterwaul!

1ST CAT: On watch day and night, no chance of a sly catnap.

CALICO: Alright! Alright! I give in; just pack in the cat banter before I go catatonic. And before you ask, yes, I'll smuggle plenty of catnip back in my luggage. *(PHOBIA enters; the cats react immediately, shrinking away from her and forming a group.)*

PHOBIA: Just the cats I wanted to see, isn't that lucky? Well of course it is, there must be one black cat among you. Not so lucky for you though – I could say ill met by moonlight. But don't be afraid, this is just a friendly cat call. *(A pause.)* Now, where's Calico? *(Making him out in the darkness.)* Ah, there you are. *(She lunges and takes CALICO by the scruff of his neck, taking him to the front of the stage before turning back to the others.)* You lot, keep your ears and your mouths shut – I don't want anyone letting the cat out of the bag. *(Turning to CALICO.)* Now my furry friend, I have a little proposition for you, so listen carefully. You and I are going to set sail on a ship I've hired to make a voyage to the kingdom of Barbary. We'll sail before Fitzwarren does and as we'll be travelling light, we'll arrive well before he does. Now I think about it, with his crew it's more like if he does. The only cargo we'll be carrying is my friends the rats – I think you've met them already. When we get to Barbary we'll let them ashore and I'll fix it so they cause mayhem; then you turn up in the nick of time and chase the rats away. I'll make sure they won't give you too much trouble. And when the king has fallen for our nice little scam, we'll split the reward and disappear with our ill-gotten gains. Now doesn't that sound like a good plan? I assume I can count on you? You'll be a very rich cat burglar. What do you say? *(CALICO shakes his head madly and attempts to break away. PHOBIA'S mood suddenly changes.)* No one, but no one, says no to me! You're coming on this voyage whether you like it or not. I've asked you nicely, but as you refuse you can do it the hard way. *(She calls offstage.)* Come here rats, I need you! *(SNITCH and the other rats enter. The cats, who have been watching all this time, move forward as if to intervene and PHOBIA is momentarily distracted; CALICO seizes his chance to make a run for it. PHOBIA calls to the rats.)* Get him! Don't let him escape! *(The rats set off in pursuit of CALICO, while PHOBIA holds the other cats in check. At the end of a chase, CALICO is cornered and the rats throw a net over him and take him prisoner.)* Well done boys! We've got everything we need now, so let's head to the harbour, go aboard our ship and sail with the tide! *(Curtain.)*

ACT TWO
Scene One

The town square in early morning light, which increases very slowly during this scene. ALICE and the cats are on stage.

ALICE: *(At the top of her voice.)* Wake up everyone! Wake up! Emergency! *(DICK, FITZWARREN, TAPIOCA, CAPTAIN COCKLESHELL, SALTY and the townspeople slowly enter as if suddenly awoken; yawning and putting the final touches to their clothes. The townspeople react to all that is said.)*

FITZWARREN: Now then Alice! What's all this about? Why are you waking us up at the crack of dawn?

TAPIOCA: And why are you surrounded by cats? I hope they're not dealing catnip. I'll get my catapult – that'll get rid of 'em!

ALICE: No, no! They woke me up yowling outside my window. It seems there's something terribly important they need to tell us. But I can't work out what it is.

FITZWARREN: Nonsense! What could a cat possibly have to say that we need to hear? Probably just after another rise in their milk ration.

TAPIOCA: So just give them a catlick and a promise and send them on their way.

DICK: Let me see if I can find out what's going on; let me try and talk to them.

ALICE: Thanks Dick; you're the only one who might understand them. *(DICK goes to the first cat and takes his paw.)*

DICK: Now don't be afraid, just tell me what's happened. *(The first cat meows into DICK'S ear. A pause while DICK digests this.)* He says that Phobia has done a deal with the rats and set sail for Barbary.

ALL: She's never! *(The second cat meows into DICK'S ear.)*

DICK: And she and the rats plan to make a thorough nuisance of themselves and then to trick the King into giving them a reward.

ALL: We don't believe it! *(The third cat pushes in and meows into DICK'S ear.)*

DICK: And they've gone and catnapped Calico and they're going to force him to be their secret weapon and to pretend to chase the rats away! *(After a moment's stunned silence.)*

ALL: They can't have! *(The cats nod in unison.)*

DICK: But that's awful! Are you sure? *(Again the cats nod.)* What am I going to do? What am I going to do?

ALICE: *(Taking DICK'S hand.)* Don't worry Dick, we'll rescue Calico somehow if it's the last thing we do.

FITZWARREN: Let's think about this. Whatever we do we mustn't panic.

TAPIOCA: Don't panic! Don't panic!

FITZWARREN: Listen. All we can do is set sail ourselves as soon as possible and try to warn the King as soon as we arrive. But first we still need a crew; let's see, we've got me, the Captain and Salty, and then there's Dick, Alice and Tapioca – but that's still not enough. *(Turning to the crowd.)* Who's up for an adventure? Who'll join our jolly crew?

1ST CITIZEN: I'll come!

COCKLESHELL: But what about all those pirates who plague the bounding main?

1ST CITIZEN: It would take an <u>aaar</u>mada to stop me.

2ND CITIZEN: I'll come too!

SALTY: Think of all those sea monsters!

2ND CITIZEN: That don't scare me – I've been living with a dragon for years.

3RD CITIZEN: Count me in too!

COCKLESHELL: You'll be seasick all the time.

3RD CITIZEN: Just part of life's ups and downs.

SALTY: And you won't get paid a penny.

ALL THREE: No change there then!

Act 2　　　　　　　　DICK WHITTINGTON　　　　　　　　33

TAPIOCA: And if we sink it won't be payday, it'll be mayday!

FITWARREN: Well, now we have a crew we can get going. Go and pack your things everyone and we'll meet at the harbour, ready to board the good ship The Unicorn. We'll sail with the morning tide. So follow me! No more time to waste! *(Everyone exits except DICK.)*

DICK: He makes everything sound so easy; I wish I could believe that we'd catch up with those rascally rats and that's we'd rescue Calico, safe and sound. But somehow I just can't see it happening. I'm going to miss him so much. Oh why did I think that coming to London would lead to fame and fortune? All that's happened is that I've lost the best friend I ever had. *(A pause and a decision.)* I can't stay here anymore, I've got to get away. I'll get my things and go back where I belong and try to make a new start – after all no one here will miss me. What else have I got to lose? *(He exits. The lighting is now full, broad daylight. After a pause ALICE enters.)*

ALICE: Dick! Dick! Where are you? Why didn't you follow us? *(To the audience.)* I've got a bad feeling about this; where can he be? Have you seen him?

AUDIENCE: Yes! *(But if the response subdued.)*

ALICE: I said have you seen Dick? Please tell me!

AUDIENCE: Yes!

ALICE: Don't tell me he's leaving us; he hasn't left has he?

AUDIENCE: Oh yes, he has!

ALICE: Oh no, he hasn't!

AUDIENCE: Oh yes, he has!

ALICE: I can't believe he'd do that; he couldn't, he wouldn't – we need him. We'll miss him – *(Now reflective.)* well I'll certainly miss him. *(Now determined.)* But I won't let him walk out on us like that; I'll follow him and convince him to come back to us. I know I can do it. And I think I know which way he'll have gone. Off I go – wish me luck! *(She exits.)*

Scene Two

In front of half tabs or on a lower stage. There is a large milestone which reads "Highgate Hill. Five miles to London Town". DICK enters with a small pack, containing his few belongings.

DICK: I need a rest and this is as good a place as anywhere to take a last look at London. Well good riddance! *(He sits and stares into space.)* And there I was thinking that things were looking up for us at last, that Calico and I had prospects. What a fool! And all along that horrible woman was planning to use poor Calico as a pawn in her game. I just don't understand these big city people whose only motive is money – well I've had enough. London's seen the last of me!

ALICE enters unseen by DICK.

ALICE: No it hasn't, not if I've got anything to do with it! *(DICK springs up.)*

DICK: Alice! What are you doing here? How did you find me?

ALICE: That was easy; I guessed that you'd be heading back to your old haunts, and there's only one road that will take you there. But to answer your first question, I've come to talk some sense into that head of yours. What do you think you're doing, going off like that without a word to your friends? *(ALICE becomes angry and squares up to him.)* You've walked away from Calico – you said he was your best friend. And you've walked away from me. I thought you were better than that!

DICK: But…but….

ALICE: Don't you but me! You've got a job to do; you've got to sail with us to help foil Phobia's rotten little plan – and you've got to rescue Calico before any harm comes to him. So pick up that pack of yours and come back with me – now! *(There is the distant sound of a peal of bells, which continues during the next few lines of dialogue. ALICE'S manner softens.)* Listen – do you hear those bells? Do you know which bells they are?

DICK: Yes, they're Bow Bells – I've heard them often enough.

ALICE: Good! So you know what they're saying?

DICK: I don't understand – bells don't speak.

ALICE: That's what you think. Can't you hear? They're saying "Turn again Whittington, London's your home. Turn again Whittington, no more to roam." *(The bells cease; a pause.)*

DICK: You're right to be angry with me Alice, it's the least I deserve. I don't know what got into me, giving up like that. I can't abandon Calico and I'll do whatever I can to help you and your father foil Phobia's plans. And I'm sorry for letting you down.

ALICE: That's better; that's what I needed to hear. Come on then – as I said, there's a job to be done and it won't wait! *(DICK picks up his pack and they exit hand in hand.)*

Scene Three

At sea, aboard the good ship The Unicorn. Suggestions for the set: either a rail at the back of the stage, high enough for the pirates to hide behind and then climb over or a 'ship' which the pirates 'wear' and walk up the aisle. There can either be a real ship's rail at the front of the stage or an imaginary one, depending on the set chosen. On stage are DICK, FITZWARREN, ALICE, TAPIOCA, CAPTAIN COCKLESHELL, SALTY and the CREW.

DICK: This is the life! I never thought I'd have the chance to sail the bounding main in search of adventure. *(To FITZWARREN.)* Thank you for giving me the chance.

FITZWARREN: Well I'm glad you're enjoying yourself, but to me this is all in a day's work.

ALICE: And it's lovely to be in the fresh air; it makes a pleasant change from smelly old London Town. I can feel it doing me good.

TAPIOCA: And there's me thinking my nose had gone on strike.

FITZWARREN: *(To ALICE.)* That's good, but don't forget you're supposed to be on watch now.

ALICE: Sorry Father; I'll get back to my post. *(She goes to the rail, at the back or front of the stage depending on the set, and begins to scan the horizon.)*

TAPIOCA: Well I'm not having any fun. We're running out of grub and it's not good for me being on short rations.

DICK: Six slices of bacon, four eggs, three sausages and a dozen ship's biscuits for brekky doesn't sound like short rations to me.

TAPIOCA: And I'm bored. We've been sailing for days and we're getting nowhere; there's not nearly enough wind.

DICK: *(Aside.)* You're not standing where I am.

TAPIOCA: And another thing! I think we're miles off course. *(Pointing at CAPTAIN COCKLESHELL and SALTY.)* These two don't have a clue when it comes to navigation. The only chart they can read is the Top Twenty.

Act 2 DICK WHITTINGTON 37

COCKLESHELL: That's hardly fair! We know exactly where we are, we navigate by the stars.

TAPIOCA: In that case with your knowledge of the heavens, we'll end up in Neverland.

SALTY: Anyway, what makes you think we're off course?

TAPIOCA: Cos we're going round and round in circles. *(She looks over the rail facing the audience.)* I've definitely seen those waves before; I'd recognise them anywhere.

COCKLESHELL: Recognise waves? You must be joking!

TAPIOCA: It's a joke you want is it? Then try this one for size. What lies at the bottom of the sea and shivers?

SALTY: I don't know; what lies at the bottom of the sea and shivers?

TAPIOCA: A nervous wreck! *(General groans.)*

COCKLESHELL: Oh, very funny I don't think!

ALICE: *(Shouting.)* Ship ahoy! Ship ahoy! *(Everyone turns to her.)* This is no joke – there's ship bearing down on us fast; and it looks like it's going to come alongside.

SALTY: *(Clapping the wrong end of a telescope to his eye.)* Don't worry, she's miles away; she'll never catch us.

FITZWARREN: *(Snatching the telescope.)* Idiot! Let me have a look! *(He peers through the telescope either to the back of the stage or out to the audience, depending on the set.)*

DICK: Can you see her flag? Is she friend or foe?

ALICE: I've got a bad feeling about this; she seems determined to overtake us.

FITZWARREN: I'm afraid you're right, Alice; she's a pirate ship – she's flying the Jolly Roger, and the crew look really fierce.

TAPIOCA: Don't panic! Don't panic!

DICK: Then we must prepare to repel boarders. *(To COCKLESHELL.)* Where do you keep the swords and pistols? Quickly man!

COCKLESHELL: *(To SALTY.)* You were loading the ship – where did you put them?

SALTY: Me? I didn't put them anywhere; I thought you were in charge of the swords and pistols.

TAPIOCA: Oh, great; now we really should panic!

FITZWARREN: You useless pair! If these pirates want to make you walk the plank then I'll help them!

DICK: No swords, no pistols? We've got nothing to fight with.

COCKLESHELL: We've still got Tapioca – she's the ultimate deterrent!

DICK: No, no – we'll just have to fight them with our bare hands.

ALICE: That's very brave, Dick – but it's hopeless. You'll be cut to pieces.

FITZWARREN: Alice is right – we've no option but to surrender. Anyway, it's too late. *(Depending on the choice of set, either: we see sails and a Jolly Roger appear behind the ship's rail or the pirates 'ship' comes down the aisle and 'comes alongside' the stage.)*

BLACK BERRY: *(From behind the rail or from the 'ship'.)* Get 'em, me hearties! *(The pirates scramble over the rail or onto the stage from the 'ship'.)*

PIRATES: *(All together, once on board.)* Arrr, arrr, arrr!

TAPIOCA: What sort of language is that?

BLACK BERRY: That be pirate speak; don't you know that to err is human, but to arrr is to talk pirate! *(Looking about him.)* Well, well, what do we have here? Looks like a good haul boys; not sure about the cargo but this lot should fetch a pretty penny when we sell them as slaves to the King of Barbary! Especially these two. *(Indicating ALICE and TAPIOCA.)*

FITZWARREN: Barbary? But that's where we're heading.

BLACK BERRY: Well, isn't that just hunky-dory? We can give you a lift.

Act 2   DICK WHITTINGTON   39

ALICE: *(Sarcastically.)* Well that's kind offer, but I don't think we'll come; we haven't been introduced. We don't even know your name.

DICK: As he's a pirate it has to be something really sinister. Let me see, it's got to be black something. Black Beard? No, that's been taken. Black Jack? That'd be a bit of a gamble. Black Mark? Wouldn't look good on his piraty CV.

BLACK BERRY: If you must know, it's Black Berry! *(Everyone laughs, including the pirates. BLACK BERRY glares at them.)*

TAPIOCA: *(Taking a liking to him.)* Oh, so you're a fruity pirate? Just my type; I've known lots of pirates and you don't frighten me. I knew one who'd been shot at so often he needed a hook and a wooden leg. Cost him a fortune – he paid an arm and a leg for them. *(More groans.)* I knew another one who wore a great gold earring; I asked him how much it cost and he said a back and ear! *(Yet more groans.)*

BLACK BERRY: *(To TAPIOCA.)* I'm beginning to like the cut of your jib. Maybe I won't sell you into slavery; you can come with me when I go on holiday – I could do with a bit of arrr and arrr!

DICK: I'm curious; I've heard that pirates are great ones for singing – sea shanties and all that. Must help to pass the time during all those months at sea.

BLACK BERRY: Indeed we are – we're famous for hitting the high cs.

PIRATES: We're always in harrrmony! Listen! *(They sing the line "Don't cry for me Arrrgentina".)*

ALICE: What, don't you ever fall out over splitting the loot?

BLACK BERRY: No, we never arrrgue....

PIRATES: We always see aye to aye!

FITZWARREN: Enough! Enough! In that case, can I suggest we make a deal that will allow you all to make a lot more money than selling us into slavery, with no risk to life and limb?

BLACK BERRY: Go on – I'm listening.

FITZWARREN: I'll give you the whole story later, but if our plan comes off we're in line for a big reward from the King of Barbary. If you and your crew will help us, we'll split it fifty-fifty. Just help us to navigate to Barbary and we'll do the rest.

BLACK BERRY: Well the arrrithmetic stacks up; how about it boys?

PIRATES: Nice arrangement!

BLACK BERRY: Arrrgreed! Back to the ship boys – we'll throw these landlubbers a line and tow them to Barbary! (*The crew either go back over the rail, or into their 'ship' and exit down the aisle as the curtains close.*)

Act 2   DICK WHITTINGTON   41

Scene Four

Below decks on The Unicorn; in front of half tabs or on the lower stage. TAPIOCA and some of the pirates enter.

TAPIOCA: *(To the audience.)* Hello everyone!

AUDIENCE: Hello! *(And then if the response is subdued.)*

TAPIOCA: Is there anyone out there? I said hello!

AUDIENCE: Hello!

TAPIOCA: That's better, I can hear you now. Well, now that the boss has done a deal with Black Berry and his boys, we're all friends and we're on our way to Barbary. But I'm sooo bored with looking at sea, nothing but sea. What I need is some entertainment. Don't say it – so do you! Now these pirates claim to be good singers, so I've asked them to give you a little song. *(To the PIRATES.)* Well come on boys – off you go! *(TAPIOCA joins the pirates in singing a short, jolly, pirate related song. As usual, inspiration for this can be found on the internet. As the song ends.)* Well, that was lovely – I don't think. *(To the audience.)* But now it's your turn; the words are in your programme. So altogether now, one, two, three! *(TAPIOCA and the pirates lead the audience in the song, which can be repeated according to audience reaction. When the song finishes.)* Thank you audience, we really enjoyed that. It's helped to pass the time so fast that next time we see you all, we'll be in the Kingdom of Barbary. So ta ta for now! *(TAPIOCA and the PIRATES exit.)*

Scene Five

> *The court of Boho, the King of Barbary who is prone to behave as a spoilt child and who, perhaps, is the epitome of hippie-chic. On stage are the KING, his COURTIERS and PHOBIA dragging CALICO, who's paws are bound.*

PHOBIA: *(Somewhat grovelling.)* Greetings, your majesty; we are deeply honoured to be admitted to your august presence. We have journeyed many days, through storms and dangers.....

BOHO: *(Interrupting.)* Yes, yes! So you've had a difficult journey – I've heard it all before! What I really want to know is what have you brought me in the way of presents? Every visitor is expected to bring me goodies, lots and lots of goodies. So what have you brought? Gold? Jewels? Statues? Spices? Slaves? The latest fashions? All of them?

PHOBIA: None of those I'm afraid your majesty.

BOHO: Well what have you brought me? Answer me!

PHOBIA: Nothing. *(The courtiers look horrified – this is obviously a bad move.)*

BOHO: Nothing! Then I have nothing more to say to you! Leave now or it will be the worse for you.

PHOBIA: Your majesty, I may bring you no presents but I and this cat can do you a great service. *(CALICO is trying to pull away, but PHOBIA does not yield an inch.)*

BOHO: You and that cat! What can you possibly do for me? Answer me that!

PHOBIA: We can rid your court of all those rats.

BOHO: Rats! Rats? There are no rats here.

PHOBIA: On the contrary – your court is overrun with rats. Look, here are some now! *(SNITCH and the rats swagger in; the KING and courtiers draw back in alarm.)*

SNITCH: *(With an exaggerated bow.)* Good day to you, majesty. We do so like your court – the larders are particularly good. *(The rats rub their stomachs.)* Pity they're empty now – and of course so are your wine cellars. And we do like the beds, don't we lads? *(The rats nod in agreement.)* Very comfy, but you might want to change the sheets.

BOHO: How dare you! I'll, I'll…..

SNITCH: Yeah? What'll you do? You won't find it so easy to get rid of us, 'eh boys? *(The rats nod once more.)* We're here to stay!

PHOBIA: And that's where I and this cat come in. I told you we could do you a service; I'll set this cat on the rats for you – he'll chase them away, no problem.

SNITCH: *(He and the rats drop to their knees, raising their hands in supplication.)* Oh no, lady! Anything but that; spare us. Please don't set the nasty, cruel cat on us!

PHOBIA: *(To BOHO.)* See, problem solved; just one little detail – how much will you pay me to get rid of these rats? *(A pause.)* On second thoughts, a thousand gold pieces should do it.

BOHO: A thousand gold pieces? That's, that's…. daylight robbery!

PHOBIA: It's a thousand or no deal.

BOHO: Oh, very well! Just get rid of these rats!

PHOBIA: I thought you'd see sense. In that case, here we go! *(She frees CALICO'S paws and releases her grip on him.)* Now, get to work! Sort out these rats!

RATS: *(Getting up and starting to shake.)* Please, please don't hurt us! *(CALICO crosses his paws and stands stock still.)*

PHOBIA: *(Pushing CALICO.)* What are you waiting for, you feeble feline furball? Get on with it, or it's the worse for you! *(CALICO still does not move.)* I'll tie your tail in knots and pull your whiskers!

BOHO: *(To PHOBIA as the light slowly dawns.)* Just one little moment! I have the distinct feeling that you and these rats are working together; you've planned to invade my court and trick me out of the reward money. Yes that's it, isn't it? *(Coming to CALICO.)* Tell me cat, are this woman and these rats trying to trick me? *(CALICO emphatically nods agreement. BOHO turns to PHOBIA.)* You'll pay for this! But now I see I have a problem – oh who will rid me of these turbulent rats?

DICK: *(Entering with FITZWARREN, TAPIOCA, ALICE, CAPTAIN COCKLESHELL, SALTY, the CREW and BLACK BERRY and the PIRATES.)* We will! Or rather my friend the cat will! *(Going to CALICO.)* Your majesty, you're right in thinking that they've plotted to trick you out of the reward money. *(To CALICO.)* Well done for refusing to work for Phobia – will you do some work for me? *(CALICO nods.)* Then get them like you did before! *(CALICO rubs his paws in anticipation, ideally showing his claws.)*

SNITCH: This means trouble boys! Run! Run for your lives! I'm deserting this sinking ship, and if you've got any sense you will too!

PHOBIA: Count me in on that – I'm coming with you! *(CALICO launches himself at the rats, who flee in terror down the aisle, closely followed by PHOBIA.)*

DICK: *(As she goes.)* Good riddance, you ratbag! *(There are a few moments of silence as everyone watches the rats and PHOBIA disappear, then BOHO and the courtiers applaud CALICO'S efforts. He takes a bow in acknowledgement.)*

BOHO: Well done! Well done! You've saved us.

DICK: Yes, well done my friend. *(Putting an arm round Calico.)* Thank goodness we've found you – I've missed you so much.

ALICE: *(Taking his paws.)* And so have I; you're our hero!

FITZWARREN: And I'm glad we've found you too; in fact I'm so impressed that I'm appointing you chief rat catcher on all my ships.

TAPIOCA: That's when you're not busy keeping them out of my pantry.

BOHO: Well it appears that I have another set of travellers invading my court unasked – but I'm glad that you did. Now, what have you brought me?

FITZWARREN: Everything you could possible want! Fur coats for those cold winter nights; umbrellas for those April showers; Chili peppers to put a bit of spice in your life....

TAPIOCA: I could do with some of that – things have been really dull lately.

FITZWARREN: Oh yes, and some coal, blankets and ice skates; I'm sure you'll find it all very useful with weather like yours.

BOHO: It seems you have something to learn about our climate; but no matter – I'm so grateful to you all that I'll buy all your cargo and give you the thousand gold pieces I was going to give to that horrible woman. Are you happy with that? *(All the travellers nod their approval.)*

FITZWARREN: Indeed we are your majesty! You are very generous and it's all we could have hoped for. *(Turning to DICK.)* Well Dick, your share of the profits means you're now a very rich man. What do you plan to do now?

DICK: Why, stay with you of course. *(Going to ALICE and taking her hands.)* But first I have to ask Alice a question. *(To ALICE.)* I wouldn't have dared ask you when I had no money, but now that I can look after you properly things have changed – will you have me as your husband? That's assuming your father approves.

ALICE: Yes, of course; you've made me the happiest girl in the world!

FITZWARREN: And you both have my blessing.

ALL: Hurrah!

DICK: But I don't have a ring to give you...

ALICE: Don't worry, let me give you this. Wear it and it will always remind you of me. *(She take takes a necklace with a small symbol from around her neck and hands it to DICK.)* It's all I had with me when I went to the orphanage and I've treasured it ever since; it must have belonged to my mother.

TAPIOCA: *(Catching sight of the necklace.)* 'Ere wait a minute! Let me see that! *(DICK hands it to her.)* I recognise this – it's the only thing I could give my little girl before they put me in the poorhouse, 'cos I couldn't pay me bills.

ALICE: But that means...

TAPIOCA: Yes, I'm your mum and you're my long lost daughter! Come here and give me a cuddle! *(They embrace.)*

ALICE: *(Breaking away.)* Now I'm even happier, if that's possible. First a husband, now a mother; two miracles in one day!

DICK: Oh goody! I've just acquired a mother-in-law. Lucky me!

BLACK BERRY: *(Coming forward.)* All this talk of happiness has got me thinking and now I'm after a different sort of treasure. *(To TAPIOCA.)* How about you and me getting together and turning our pirate ship into a cruise ship? We can all go straight and still make a fortune – what d'you say?

TAPIOCA: I say hello shipmate! *(The pirates cheer.)*

BLACK BERRY: *(Turning to CAPTAIN COCKLESHELL and SALTY.)* Mind you, I wouldn't trust you two to crew a pedalo but you can be in charge of on board entertainment; you'll certainly give the passengers something to laugh at. How does that suit you?

COCKLESHELL: I can see us now, playing the music and doing all the announcements.

SALTY: Yeah! We can call it pirate radio!

BOHO: It seems that your lives are now mapped out and everyone's happy; so before you all set sail for your homeland I think we should celebrate. So, let's celebrate!

ALL: Let's celebrate!

Closing songs, walkdown and final curtain.

www.ingramcontent.com/pod-product-compliance
Lightning Source LLC
Chambersburg PA
CBHW071548080526
44588CB00011B/1826